CARING FOR YOUR GOLDFISH

How to care for your Goldfish and everything
you need to know to keep them well

WRITTEN BY VETERINARY EXPERT

DR. GORDON ROBERTS BVSC MRCVS

Hello! My name is Gordon Roberts and I'm the author of this book. I hope you enjoy all of the specialist advice it contains. I'm a huge advocate of preventative care for animals, and I'd love to see more pet owners taking the time to research their pet's health care needs.

Being proactive and educating yourself about your pet's health now, rather than later on, could save you and your pet a lot of trouble in the long run.

If you'd like to read more of my professional pet care advice simply go to my website at http://drgordonroberts.com/freereportsdownload/.

As a thank you for purchasing this book, you'll find dozens of bonus pet care reports there to download and keep, absolutely free of charge!

Best wishes,

Gordon
Founder, Wellpets

Contents

~

Introduction

~

Welcome to the wonderful world of the goldfish enthusiast. Goldfish are beautiful, relatively easy to keep and don't cost the earth. This makes them one of the most popular small pets in the world. Goldfish have been kept by humans for centuries, but not always correctly. Gone are the days when a simple goldfish bowl and tap water will suffice – goldfish care has changed considerably now that science has taught us the complexity of these creatures.

We now know that they need very specific water conditions to survive and thrive in, including water that is the right temperature and pH. They also need an aquarium with a large enough surface area to oxygenate the water, or they will not do well. This is one reason why today's goldfish fans never keep their fish in goldfish bowls – they are the wrong shape and size to keep healthy goldfish in.

Don't worry if you're feeling daunted by all of this information - this book will bring you up to speed with modern goldfish keeping methods, and show you the right tricks and procedures for keeping healthy goldfish. We've made sure to avoid obscure terminology so you will find it very easy and straightforward to understand.

Bearing in mind that goldfish can live for ten years or more (and have been found to live for up to 40 years in rare cases) you will need to know as much as you can about looking after your new water babies. We hope that after reading this book you and your finned friends have a long and happy future together. Are you ready? Good - let's begin!

Chapter 1
Goldfish history and biology

Goldfish have been kept as pets for centuries, but have you ever wondered where they came from? Well, it's thought that the humble but beautiful goldfish is descended from a fish called the Prussian Carp which comes from Eastern and South Eastern Asia. These fish are part of a group called the Cyprinidae family. The wild varieties of these fish still exist today in the rivers and lakes of Asia.

Goldfish history

References to goldfish can be found in Chinese poetry that dates back to 800AD. It's thought that about a thousand years ago, in the Song era, people in China began to breed carp, at first just for food but later on for decorative reasons in watergardens and ornamental ponds. We know that the first of these domesticated carp was grey in colour, but that over time, some colour mutations were produced by breeders which included the orange that we see in many of today's pet fish. There were also yellow varieties - these were only kept by royalty because yellow was the traditional royal colour.

In the early 16th century, the popularity of these goldfish spread to Japan where two new varieties were developed: the Tosakin goldfish, which has a beautiful fanned tail and has been depicted in many Japanese paintings, and the Ryukin goldfish, with its distinctive pointed head.

Fast forward to the 17th century and the goldfish was becoming popular in Europe, where their metallic scales turned them into a symbol of good fortune. At first they were a rarity, and were given as presents for one year wedding anniversaries, as a sign of prosperity to come. Later on in the 1850s they arrived in America and the rest of the world followed.

The beautiful colourings of goldfish and their resilience as pets meant that their popularity soon became widespread. However, their resilience has been both a blessing and a curse – for a long time, people gave bags of goldfish away as prizes at fairgrounds and this led to a lot of fish going to ill-equipped homes. Somewhere along the way, it became the norm for these fish to be kept in small round goldfish bowls which had a smaller surface area of water and didn't provide enough oxygen for the fish. Luckily today's goldfish keepers are a bit more savvy and most fish can be found in aquariums where they have lots of space to swim and plenty of underwater plants and accessories.

Goldfish biology

Wild goldfish or carp can grow to a foot long and are a dull olive brown colour. They may have barbels on their lips and have a long dorsal fin. Goldfish can also grow to a similar size if they have a big

enough environment to thrive in, but since most pet goldfish are kept in tanks and smaller ponds, they won't grow to their full size.

Some goldfish have been reintroduced to the wild, mostly by people who can no longer keep them. When this happens, the domesticated goldfish can breed with their wild cousins and within three generations, the gold colour has disappeared and the goldfish from that breeding line are back to their original olive colouring.

Here are some interesting facts for you about the goldfish's biology:

Goldfish don't have stomachs, and instead use their intestines to digest their food. This makes them prone to digestive problems if they are fed the wrong diet, and overfeeding can be very harmful to them. They need to be fed in small amounts rather than one huge meal every day.

Goldfish live a long time. For such small creatures, these pets can live for ten to fifteen years if looked after properly. Some fish have been known to live twice as long.

Goldfish have longer memories than you think. The saying that goldfish have a three second memory is wrong. Scientists have found that fish can remember things for three months or so. They can even recognise faces and colours.

Goldfish can't close their eyes. You might think that your goldfish never sleeps – but he does! He just does it with his eyes open.

Goldfish respond to light levels by being more colourful. Fish that are kept outdoors in natural sunlight have been found to develop more colourful scales than those kept in darker environments.

Goldfish have a protective layer of slime. So be careful not to touch your goldfish or you could rub off this layer, which acts as a barrier to infections.

Chapter 2:
Types of goldfish

Today's goldfish come in dozens of different varieties, but there are about eighteen really popular types that you will come across in pet shops. This section will describe these in brief, so that you can learn to recognise them.

Goldfish breeds and varieties

Today the goldfish is no longer just a golden scaled fish. In fact, these fishes can be vastly different from each other, depending on what variety or breeding line they come from. Many varieties were bred in Japan and China and can have anything from bulging eyes to long fanned tails. However, not all varieties will live in harmony together so if you are planning to have a mixed aquarium you will need to research which are the best varieties to live together. There are about 300 different varieties of goldfish across the world. To start you off, here is a beginner's guide to the most popular types of goldfish you will come across.

Common

The common goldfish, as the name suggests, is the original variety with no weird or wonderful mutations. This fish has a single tail with a flat, elongated body. They are the hardiest of all the goldfish, having not been subjected to selective breeding methods. As such, they're really good for beginners because they eat almost anything they are given and, if cared for properly, they can live for a long time. Commons also come in a range of colours from the standard orange-gold, white, black, chocolate, and yellow.

Comet

Comets come from the USA, where they were first developed in the 1880s. These little fish are similar to their Common cousins but with a more elongated tail and a slightly smaller size. These fish are very active and do well in large environments where they can race about to their heart's desire. They are also hardy and can survive easily in outdoor ponds. They come in red, orange, white and yellow, as well as red and white.

Shubunkin

Shubunkin (or calico coloured) goldfish are also single tailed fish, but they come with pearly scales which have an opalescent appearance because they are a mixture of transparent and metallic colours. They come from Japan, where they were bred with a variety of colours including a mixture of grey, white, blue, red and chocolate. In general, single-tailed fish like the Common, the Comet and the Shubunkin don't mix well in aquariums with twin-tailed varieties which are slower and less agile.

Black Moor

As the name suggests, Black Moor goldfish have dramatic black colouring and egg shaped bodies. They also have large bulging eyes on either side of their head. Despite their very prominent eyes, these fish have poor eyesight and are better off kept in tanks rather than large ponds. One fascinating thing about Black Moors is that they can turn back to an orange-gold colour if kept in warmer water.

Bubble eye

Like the Black Moor, the Bubble Eye goldfish have poor vision but they make up for this with their dramatic looks. They have fluid filled sacks under each eye and their eyes point upwards. These sacs are fragile and can get ruptured if the fish is injured in a fight or a collision. Because of this you will need a tank with no sharp objects or fake plants. Bubble Eyes can't compete for food with faster fish like the Common, so they are best kept with other slower twin tails.

Celestial eye

The Celestial Eye has been given the nickname "the stargazer" and this is because the eyes turn upwards towards the heavens. Like the Bubble Eye fish, these are not recommended for beginners as they are more delicate and need a little bit more care to maintain. Celestials can't see their food very well so they need more time to feed and will not thrive if there are faster fish in the tank.

Fantail

Fantail goldfish have beautiful fanned twin tails and rounded egg shaped bodies, making them very pleasing to the eye. They are a hardy fish variety and can live for ten years or more. They come with three types of scales: matt white scales, solid metallic orange scales and speckled scales.

Lionchu

The Lionchu comes from Thailand and is the result of cross-breeding a Lionhead with a Ranchu. They have the enlarged heads of their Lionhead cousins but without the dorsal fin. These fish are slower movers and only do well with other twin-tailed varieties. They come in a range of colours including bi-colours such as red-and-white.

Lionhead

The Chinese Lionhead is very cute and one of the most widely kept types of goldfish – also being amongst the oldest varieties. The curved back and egg shaped body and the enlarged flesh on the head (known as the wen) gives this fish a very distinctive toy-like appearance. This is another fish that can have poor eyesight, and as such it isn't recommended for beginners.

Oranda

Like the Lionhead, the Oranda has a "wen" or hood that grows on its head, giving it the same raspberry shaped appearance. The Oranda is

born without the wen, which only develops as the fish reaches maturity. The wen itself is prone to bacterial infections so it should always be examined for signs of poor health. When it overgrows, the eyes can be concealed leading to poor eyesight. Still, the Oranda is a very popular choice with goldfish enthusiasts.

Panda Moor

With protruding eyes similar to the Moor goldfish, the Panda Moor has one delightful difference; it comes in a black-and-white colour just like the Panda bear it is named after. A relatively new breed, these twin-tailed fish are slower with poorer eyesight than some goldfish, and as such they need to be kept with similar breeds in order to thrive.

Pearlscale

Pearlscale fish have very unusual scales that are raised with dark outlines and lighter centres, making it look like they have tiny pearls under their skin. This makes them a very unique type of goldfish. They have very rounded bodies which hinder their swimming efforts and make it a little bit harder for them to compete with other fish for food.

Pompom

These funny looking but endearing fish, have pompom-like growths coming from their noses. These fish are for more experienced aquarium keepers, as the nose pompoms can get damaged in the wrong environment. Like the rest of their twin-tailed companions, they are slower moving fish. They come in a wide variety of colours.

Ranchu

These Japanese fish look a bit like Lionheads, but they have shorter turned in tails and arched backs. The larger head, rounded body and beautiful bi-colours are its most distinctive features. These fish are highly regarded in their native Japan.

Ryukin

These fish are very similar to their fantail cousins, but with a very high arched back. They are active, which makes them very popular. These egg shaped fish are prone to swim bladder disorder if they are fed too much protein. This results in them becoming constipated and flipping over. A varied diet is key to avoiding this.

Telescope eye

Telescope Eye goldfish have a curious look about them that is enhanced by their large eyes, which protrude from their bodies in the shape of small telescopes. They are born with normal eyes, but develop their telescopes at about six months to a year old. They have bodies very similar to fantails, and come in a wide range of colours including a rare black-and-white variant.

These are just some of the many varieties of goldfish you will see in aquariums around the world. Visit your local aquatic centre to see them for yourself, and choose your favourites.

Chapter 3:
Preparing to keep goldfish

Now that you know more about the goldfish and its fascinating background, it's time to start thinking about preparations for your new pet. This chapter will go through a few things you need to think about beforehand.

Before you get your goldfish

Although goldfish seem like a relatively "low maintenance" pet, you still need to be prepared for the added responsibility that comes with caring for another living thing. Here are some important questions to ask yourself before you rush out to purchase your goldfish:

- Can you afford an aquarium, fish food, accessories, veterinary care and any other expenses involved in getting goldfish?
- Do you have a suitable room in your home to keep your goldfish, away from hazards, direct sunlight and other pets?
- If you're away from home a lot, who is going to look after your goldfish?
- Will there be someone at home to feed your goldfish every day, without fail?
- Are you aware that goldfish can live for well past ten years - if looked after properly?

How many goldfish should I buy?

If you're a beginner and you've never kept goldfish before, it's a good idea to start small and once you get more confident, you can add to your aquarium over time.

It's perfectly ok to keep a single goldfish if you prefer, as there is no evidence to suggest that goldfish get lonely. However, like all creatures, they will be happier in a more stimulating environment and having other fish around can certainly help with that. Whether you buy one fish to start with or a handful, is up to you. Just make sure that the tank is the right size for them, and that all the fish are compatible varieties.

Which types of goldfish can live together?

Many first time aquarium keepers get excited at the prospect of keeping a dazzling array of different fish. In reality, you need to be very careful about which fish are going to live together in the tank. If the fish varieties are too different they can end up eating each other's food, leaving some slower or poor sighted fish at a real disadvantage. Here are some general guidelines for beginners:

Fast moving, single-tailed goldfish varieties such as the Common goldfish and the Comet goldfish should always be kept with others of their kind, and should never be put in a tank with "fancy" goldfish that are slower and less able to compete for food. "Fancy" goldfish are fish that have been bred with special characteristics such as protruding eyes, very rounded bodies or head shapes, and twin-tails. These mutations, whilst attractive, put them at a slight physical disadvantage to their single-tailed counterparts. Confused? If you go back to our list of goldfish varieties in Chapter 2, you'll see that the first three goldfish on the list are fast-moving single-tailed fish (the Common, Comet and Shubunkin) and the others are all "fancy" fish that are not quite as agile. The general rule is not to mix the two groups of goldfish in the same tank.

Can goldfish live with other types of fish?

In theory, the answer is yes. If the other fish need similar living conditions (cold water temperatures) and are neither too big to be a threat to your goldfish, nor too small to be eaten by them, then they could be tank mates. However, trying to combine very different species of fish is not recommended and can cause both species unnecessary stress. You are much better off keeping goldfish with other goldfish, and getting a separate tank if you want to try keeping other types of fish.

How big should my fish tank be?

One important thing to consider is the size of your fish tank. How many fish is it designed for? One of the biggest mistakes you can make is trying to put too many fish in a tank that is too small. Fish, like any other animal kept in captivity, need space to move about in order to be happy and healthy. An overcrowded fish tank is going to pollute the water very quickly, leading to health issues for your fish. Goldfish produce a lot of ammonia as natural waste product, but if this builds up it can be toxic. These are just some of the reasons why your aquarium needs to be a decent size.

Here are some others:
- The larger the tank, the less often you will need to change the water (water changes are stressful for your fish as they change the

temperature)

- Larger tanks will maintain a more consistent water temperature (small tanks of water will change temperature rapidly if the room is particularly hot, or if someone has forgotten to close a window).
- Larger tanks mean you can create a more interesting and visually appealing aquarium
- Larger tanks mean that if you want to, you could add more fish at a later stage

At an absolute minimum, one fish should have a 20 gallon tank, and then for each additional tank you need to add another 10 gallons for fancy fish and 20 gallons for fast-moving Comets and Commons.

You might see fancy hexagonal tanks on your shopping trips, but the classic rectangular tank is the better option. It provides a nice long run for your fish to swim, a large surface area for oxygen, and a simple shape for cleaning out.

Getting a small tank, although it will be the cheapest option, will only lead to unhealthy or dying fish in the long run. So, get the largest tank you can afford – you will be very happy that you did.

Can I keep my fish in a goldfish bowl?

No. Goldfish bowls used to be the norm, but experts have proven that they are, in fact, very cruel because they don't provide enough surface area for the required oxygen levels that fish need. Aside from that goldfish bowls tend to be far too small for fish to live in.

What you need to buy

Your goldfish tank is going to be your biggest expense, but it won't be the only thing you need to invest in. Here is a list of other things you will need before you bring your goldfish home:

Gravel: for the bottom of the tank. Before adding gravel, make sure you rinse it thoroughly and remove any parts that are very sharp, to avoid injuries to your fish. The gravel on the base of the tank needs to be about 2-3 inches thick, at the very least.

Ornaments and rocks: these provide hiding places and also decoration for the tank. Choose rocks that have been specially made for aquariums and don't try to use something you've found in the garden or at the beach (these can add new compounds to the water, changing the chemistry and potentially harming your fish). Avoid pale coloured rocks that can contain high levels of calcium, which can harden the water and harm your fish.

Plants: these can be real or fake, but real ones are less likely to have sharp edges that can harm your fish. Real plants will only thrive in a tank that has been well established with the right water composition and conditions.

A filtration system: this will keep the water a decent quality and save you a lot of cleaning. If you only have one or two fish, you shouldn't really need a filter (the gravel will act as a natural filter) but for larger groups it is a wise idea.

Goldfish food: a food that's high quality that has been manufactured specifically for goldfish

Preparing your tank

Two weeks before you buy your goldfish, you will need to set up your fish tank with everything mentioned above. This will give plenty of time for the water pH to balance out and for the tank to build up some friendly bacteria. Friendly bacteria helps to convert the ammonia that your fish excrete into nitrate, which is a less harmful substance. During this time, any debris in the water caused by the accessories or gravel will settle, and the water will have time to become oxygenated.

What temperature should the water be?

Goldfish thrive in a water temperature that is between 18 to 22 degrees Celsius. You can use a thermometer to check the temperature on a regular basis. It may help to move the aquarium to a different area of the house if you're finding the temperature is too high or low.

Water quality

As you can probably guess, the health of your fish is going to depend on the quality of water you provide them with. A lot of tap water contains chlorine which is not a natural substance for fish to live in. So, if you can provide your fish with water that hasn't been chlorinated, so much the better. Lots of aquarium owners use special water conditioning treatments, which help to remove toxins and also help to maintain the fish's slimy scale coating, which protects it from harmful substances. You can buy this conditioner at your local pet shop or aquatic specialist.

The other thing to try if you are really serious about creating the optimum environment for your fish is an aquarium testing kit, which can tell you whether the water is the right pH, and whether there are harmful levels of ammonia and nitrates in the tank. You can also buy these testing kits at pet shops, or online.

Where should I put my fish tank?

The placement of your fish tank is very important to the well-being of your little fish. Choose the wrong spot and they could be vulnerable to all sorts of stressful stimuli or uncomfortable environmental factors.

Here are some tips for finding the right placement:
* A room that's not too noisy or busy with vibrations
* A good raised spot that will make it easy to a) observe your fish and b) lift the aquarium when the time comes for cleaning
* Away from open windows, direct sunlight and heaters, where possible
* Away from fumes, cooking smells and vapours, harmful cleaning sprays and aerosols, and smoke
* A place that tends to maintain a constant temperature, rather than lots of fluctuation

Chapter 4:
Choosing your goldfish, and bringing them home

So, you've bought all the necessary equipment and have had your tank set up for two weeks. Now for the exciting part – it's time to go and pick up your fish. This chapter will guide you through the process of choosing the right fish, and introducing them to their new aquarium.

Where to get your goldfish

Now that the you are ready to go and buy your goldfish, it's time for a little bit of shopping around. There are a few different places you can look for goldfish – remember that different places will have different varieties, so that will probably be a major factor in your decision. Another factor will be how healthy the fish look once you get there, and how knowledgeable the staff or breeders are when you meet them. Here are some possible places to get your goldfish:

Pet shops

Most pet shops in your local town or city will sell goldfish. But not all of them will be from good breeding lines and reputable sources, and not all of them will have been kept in great condition. Bear in mind that some of the larger pet retailers will be putting profit first, which often comes at the expense of animal welfare. Go and visit the pet shop and look out for overcrowded tanks, or fish that seem ill. If you see any evidence of this, choose somewhere else to get your fish from. Many of the smaller, independent pet shops will have more time to dedicate to the pets in their care, and may be more enthusiastic about the welfare of the creatures they sell.

Breeders or goldfish enthusiasts

Most home breeders of goldfish are very passionate about their hobby, and since goldfish don't tend to fetch a huge profit, their hearts are more than likely in the right places when it comes to looking after their fish. Spend some time chatting to a goldfish breeder and you'll soon get an idea of how knowledgeable they are and how much they care about what they do. A good breeder should have large, un-crowded tanks, clean water, filtration systems, and healthy looking fish. To find a good breeder, look up your local goldfish association or breeder's club and they should be able to provide you with a list of breeders who keep your chosen goldfish variety.

Online fisheries

Surprisingly, there are many successful online goldfish merchants where you can order your chosen varieties of fish. Make sure you choose one that explains the delivery process and sends a professional courier to deliver the fish. If you're going to go down this route, look for reviews and testimonials from the vendor beforehand.

How to choose a healthy looking fish

If you're going to be choosing your fish in person, here is a quick checklist to use that will help you to establish that the fish you have chosen are healthy:

- The goldfish is active, not lethargic
- The goldfish is neither hovering on the surface, nor sitting at the bottom listlessly
- There are no buoyancy issues (where the fish is floating against its will)
- No signs of bullying other fish in the aquarium
- No evidence of bloating
- No missing scales, blemishes, patches of greyish film
- No shredded looking tails
- Clear looking gills with no oozing or discolouration
- No signs of debris trailing from the fish

We'll go through some common health issues with goldfish later in this book.

How to get your goldfish home safely

Now that you've found some healthy goldfish that you'd like to purchase, it's time to get them home, quickly and safely, to their new tank. Ideally, you should bring someone along with you to hold the goldfish in their bags while you drive, get your keys out, and open doors.

Here are a couple of other tips:

- Try to get home as quickly as possible because plastic bags don't provide fish with a lot of oxygen, and can easily break.
- Keep the bag out of direct sunlight which could heat up the water to dangerous levels.
- Consider bringing a small box to shelter the bag from sunlight
- Keep your car cool and air conditioned before you transport the fish

Introducing your goldfish to their new home

With the trickiest parts over, you now have one task to focus on: getting your fish gradually used to their new environment, without shock or stress.

To do this, you need to keep the fish in their bags and float the bags in the tank for about half an hour, so that the fish can adjust to the new water temperature. If the bags had oxygen specially added to them at the shop, you can leave them closed. If they didn't, you should open them to allow your fish to get some oxygen into their water.

While the bags are floating you should gradually add some water from the tank into them every five to ten minutes, so that you can slowly equalise the pH. This will make it a lot more comfortable when the fish eventually get to swim in the new tank. After this period of mixing the water, you can open the bags and release them into their new tank. Leave them to settle in for an hour or two before you try feeding them.

Why is this method important?

This method of slowly and carefully introducing your fish to their new home is standard procedure. The reason it is important is that goldfish can die from shock if they are suddenly put into a new environment.

Chapter 5:
Feeding your goldfish

And, just like that, you've become a bona fide goldfish owner! Congratulations. It's a good idea to establish a solid routine as early on as possible, where you feed your fish at the same times every day. This chapter will deal with feeding your goldfish.

Why feeding is a delicate process

Fish are opportunistic feeders, which means they will eat whenever they get the chance, regardless of when their last meal was and how hungry they might be. This makes them very prone to overfeeding – they simply don't get full! Overfeeding is dangerous for goldfish, as they don't have stomachs to digest their food in. Instead, all of the digestion takes place in their intestines. Putting too much strain on the digestion can kill your fish, as their bodies simply aren't made to process huge amounts of food at one time.

What to feed your goldfish

In the wild, goldfish or carp eat a diet of insects, microorganisms, and plant life. So when it comes to diet, your goldfish will thrive best on a variety of foodstuffs, rather than just plain old fish flakes. To start with though, your fish are going to need a primary diet of fish flakes that are specifically manufactured for goldfish. Goldfish food is typically higher in carbohydrates and lower in protein than other types of fish food. You can buy it in the form of flakes or pellets. Flakes are easier to remove from the tank if they are uneaten, whereas pellets sink to the bottom. Pellets retain more nutrients and stay fresher for longer, though some pellets may be too large for very small fish to swallow. Flakes, on the other hand, cause your goldfish to swallow air when eaten, and if this happens in large amounts it can cause bloating. Whichever you choose, make sure the food is of high quality rather than buying the cheapest stuff you can find.

This staple diet of fish food should ideally be supplemented with some other foodstuffs, to give your fish a truly balanced diet.

Here are a few things that are safe to feed your fish:
- Peas, with the shells removed
- Boiled vegetables such as small pieces of broccoli
- Live food like bloodworms and brine shrimp
- Lettuce
- Fresh seaweed

These treats should only be fed in moderation. Your goldfish should have a main diet of fish food supplemented by the occasional treat from the list above.

If you want to feed your goldfish "live" food to mimic how they would feed in the wild, bear in mind that it carries with it a small risk of infection – as with anything that comes from the wild. If you're not comfortable with this risk there are freeze-dried and frozen options you can buy instead, which will be more sterile.

How often should I feed my fish?

Rather than feed your goldfish one huge meal a day, you should ideally split their food into two separate meals. Once in the morning and once in the evening is fine, depending on your own schedule. Just make sure that there is a long enough period between feeding times.

What if I forget?

Fish are very resilient creatures and nature has designed them to be able to go without food for long periods if absolutely necessary. If your fish miss one or two meals, just resume the feeding as normal and they will be fine. You don't need to give them any extra food to make up for the lost meals – this will only make them ill.

How much should I feed them?

When it comes to feeding a certain quantity, there are a lot of mixed opinions out there. Some fish enthusiasts advocate feeding as much as the fish will eat in a two minute window, others advocate a fifteen minute window. With the risk of overfeeding, is it better to be overly cautious when it comes to this rather than be "generous" with the amount of food you give. Slowly give small pinches of food over a period of a minute or two, rather than simply adding a huge amount and walking away. Make sure there is no old food left to float around – it will only rot and pollute the water. Remove any leftovers with your net after the feeding session.

Tip: Look out for trailing poo from your fish's behind – this is a definite sign of overfeeding.

Water temperature

One thing to remember is that the lower your water temperature, the less food your fish will want to eat. This is because the cooler water will slow your fish's metabolism, and vice versa – in warmer temperatures they will want to eat more than usual. So, keeping the temperature of the tank nice and cool is one way to avoid overfeeding.

Seasonal feeding

For goldfish, seasons can mean changes in appetite and feeding habits, especially for goldfish that are kept in ponds outdoors. Here are some things to keep in mind:

Spring: your goldfish will be getting more active after the cold winter, and will have an increased appetite. Spring is the time when fish get ready for the breeding season and so your goldfish will need higher levels of protein during this time.

Summer: Your goldfish will be at their most active, but since breeding season will be over you can cut back on the protein (live food) and revert back to veg and flakes. Hot weather can sometimes make goldfish lethargic, so always check that your water temperature is nice and cool.

Autumn: As the temperature drops your fish will need slightly more food to build up their food reserves over winter (this applies to fish in ponds mostly, but you'll still see an instinctual increase in appetite in your aquarium fish).

Winter: Fish will naturally eat less in winter, and if this is the case with your fish you will need to feed them less, to avoid excess food floating around the tank. They might be a little slower and less active during this period.

Chapter 6

Taming and handling your new hamster

Your goldfish can live for ten years or more as long as they are looked after properly and stay healthy. This chapter will go through some of the common health problems you will see in goldfish and how you can spot them.

Behavioural changes

Keeping your goldfish healthy means being proactive and staying vigilant for the signs of illness. But what are the signs that something is wrong?

Here are some clues:
- A goldfish that is shaking
- Any signs of swimming strangely

- Rubbing their scales on objects in the tank
- A fish that stays at the top of the tank gasping for air
- Any abnormalities in the fins or gills

Common goldfish ailments

Here are some of the most common goldfish ailments. It's important to familiarise yourself with these so that you can act quickly if you spot them developing. Since goldfish are small, fragile creatures they can go downhill very quickly if left untreated.

So, be observant and take action when you see something untoward. You'll be glad you did. The good news is that veterinary care for goldfish tends to be cheaper than it is for other pets, so don't hesitate to see your vet if you're worried.

Swim bladder disease

One of the most talked about fish ailments, yet one that is more complex than it sounds. Swim bladder disease is not one disease but a range of issues that can happen with the fish's swim bladder, with various causes. The swim bladder is a special organ in the fish's body that helps it to swim and maintain the correct buoyancy (floatation). If a goldfish wants to swim to the surface, it will take air into its swim bladder to make it more buoyant.

If the fish wants to swim downwards, it will expel air from the swim bladder, making it sink more easily to the bottom. A very clever device! If the swim bladder is not functioning properly, you will notice your fish swimming in an odd manner, floating to the surface, swimming on one side or even swimming upside down.

Don't panic if this is the case! Swim bladder issues can be cured, and they aren't contagious. They often happen in fancy fish that have been bred with unusual body shapes.

Here are some causes of swim bladder disease:
- Constipation

31

- Swallowing too much air at the surface whilst eating
- Too much food fermenting in the gut
- Sudden changes in water temperature
- Bacterial or parasitic infections

There are a few things you can do to rule out the cause of the swim bladder issue.

Firstly, check that the water in the tank is the right temperature, and chemistry. Then, quarantine the affected fish and withhold food for about two days, to rule out a digestive issue such as constipation.

After this period you can start to feed very small pieces of green food, such as peas with the shells removed. You can also try a swim bladder treatment which should help to clear up an infection if that is what has caused the issue.

Pop eye

When your goldfish's eyes start to bulge or protrude (and he isn't a variety that is supposed to have this, like the Telescope Eye or the Black Moor for example) it is a sign of a condition called Pop Eye.

The swelling is caused by a build-up of fluid in the eye, which might look a little cloudy as a result. The fish might have impaired vision as a result, and secondary infections can occur. Common causes include bacterial infections, poor water quality and injuries to the eye.

Dropsy

This is a serious condition causing your fish to bloat excessively.

Symptoms include:
- A very swollen, ready to burst, belly
- Scales that stand out from the body like a pine cone
- Bulging eyes
- Difficulty swimming, or swimming in an odd manner

Dropsy is caused by a malfunctioning of the kidneys. When this happens, the kidneys can no longer expel water from the fish's body as it normally would, and the result is that the fish swells up with the excess fluid. Injury or infection are two causes of kidney issues. You should quarantine the affected fish and try to treat the water with antibacterial treatments, special aquarium salts which are good for the kidneys and a constant temperature of about 25 degrees. In a lot of cases, dropsy is fatal but treatment is certainly worth a try.

Fin rot

Ragged looking fins or tails can be a sign of fin rot, which is usually caused by poor water conditions. If this is the case you should take immediate action to improve your water quality, changing the water and adding a water conditioner and aquarium salts until the optimum pH is reached.

Make sure you clean everything in the tank and rinse out all the gravel. When water quality is low the fish's immune systems are lower too, and this means they can get bacterial infections. You might see them rubbing their scales on the sides of objects in the tank to relieve the irritation. You can buy treatments for fin rot at your local pet shop – just follow the instructions on the bottle carefully.

White spot

If you notice white specks on your goldfish that look like soneone has sprinkled salt on them, it is a sign of a condition called White Spot (also known as Ich or Ick). These white spots are actually tiny parasites that are feeding off your fish. They will spread to the other fish in the tank, so the affected goldfishes need to be quarantined from the others and a full deep clean of the tank and a water change will be necessary.

White spot has to enter your aquarium from an infected source, such as a newly added fish, or a piece of equipment that has previously been in a different aquarium. The condition is often fatal and must be treated quickly in order to catch it in the early stages. You can buy white spot treatments from the pet shop or your local aquatic specialist.

Fungus

An injury on your fish's body may develop a fungal infection if it does not heal properly. You will notice a greyish or white substance on parts of the fish's body if this is the case. You can buy topical treatments from the pet shop. As with all infectious diseases, make sure you do a full clean of the tank when this occurs.

Chapter 7:
Cleaning the aquarium

One of the best ways to keep your fish healthy is to maintain a clean environment for them. As tanks can be large and cumbersome, many people put off cleaning the "mammoth" task of cleaning their aquariums. But it doesn't have to be a difficult task, if done right. And because the health of your fish depends on them having a clean home, it is well worth the effort. This chapter will teach you how to do it properly.

A note about clean tanks

Whilst goldfish need a clean environment to live in, the tank should not be absolutely sterile – this can be just as detrimental to goldfish health. As we mentioned before, goldfish need a certain amount of friendly bacteria in their tanks to help convert all the ammonia they produce into a safer substance (nitrate). You will therefore need to maintain a delicate balance between having a tank that is not dirty as such, and having a tank that still has a healthy amount of good bacteria present. A testing kit will be extremely useful for this, if you don't have one already.

How often should I clean my tank?

This is an area where there are lots of mixed opinions. Lot s of people advocate cleaning their tanks once or twice a week without fail. In reality though, the amount of cleaning you do should depend on the size of the tank. A 10 gallon tank should be cleaned every two weeks, and you can add another week for every 20 gallons after that.

Do I still need to clean the tank if I have a filter?

Yes – the filter will remove debris, but it won't keep the water completely clean. As well as having a good quality filter you'll need to change the water in the aquarium too when the time comes for the periodic cleaning.

What type of filter should I get?

There are two types of filter you can buy for goldfish: one is an internal filter, which stays inside the tank, and one is an external filter located outside of the tank. External filters might be a little bit more expensive but the great thing about them is they don't take up valuable space inside the tank, and they tend to be a bit more powerful and do a better job.

Filters come in different speeds or levels – you should aim for a filter than can filter 10x the volume of water in your tank per hour. So, if you have a 40 gallon tank, you should aim for a filter system that can do 400 gallons an hour.

Note: if you are cleaning out your filter, it's very important that you clean it with water from the tank, and not tap water. This is because your filter will contain the valuable friendly bacteria that keeps your fish healthy – you don't want to accidentally rinse it away. Just give the filter sponges a gentle rinse rather than a scrub, and you should be fine.

Changing water in your aquarium

As well as having a filter system, you will also need to change a third of the water in your fish tank about once a week. You should never change all of the water in one go – this will be too much of a shock to your goldfish and will ruin the delicate ecosystem you have created for them in the aquarium. Here is the most efficient way to do it, using a specially designed aquarium vacuum or pump:

1. Turn off your water filter and any other electrical devices.
2. Place one end of the vacuum or pump hose in a bucket, and the other end in the aquarium (with the fish safely out of the way).
3. Suck the water from the tank, at the point where the gravel is. This will lift out any debris lurking in the gravel, which is also acting as a natural filter for your tank.
4. As you vacuum, move the hose around to different areas of the gravel so that the entire surface of the aquarium gravel gets a clean. Do this until a third of the water has been removed from the tank and is in the bucket.
5. Now you can take out your water filter and gently rinse off any debris that might have built up on the sponges, using the bucket full of tank water you have just extracted. Do the same for any accessories you want to wash.
6. Lastly, fill up a bucket of fresh tap water and treat it with an aquarium water conditioner before you put it in the tank. You can buy this from your local aquatic centre, and it will help to remove any chlorine or toxic metals from the water. Add the new water very slowly and gradually to the tank, so as not to shock your fish with the change in temperature.

You're done! This simple procedure should be repeated every week, and will keep your fish in good health.

Should I ever disinfect a tank?

The only time you will ever need to fully clean, scrub and disinfect a tank is if you have had a contagious disease in your aquarium, or a parasite. In those cases, you'll need to completely clean the tank, whilst keeping your fish in a different tank until everything has been fully washed, rinsed and the water has been prepared for them once more.

The same goes if the unthinkable should happen and you should lose your goldfish to a fatal disease. The entire tank and its contents will need to be thoroughly cleaned before you can use it again for new goldfish.

Chapter 8:
FAQs

Now that you've read all about caring for your goldfish, it's only natural that you have some burning questions. This section will answer some of the most frequently asked questions about goldfish care, so that you can be as well informed as possible when it comes to your new pets.

My goldfish seems to have changed colour. Can this happen?

Yes, goldfish can change colour overnight after a few hours of being in darkness. Their scales will be less bright in the morning and should brighten during the day with natural daylight. Goldfish can also change colour during the course of their lives and young fish can have a very different colour to that which they attain in adulthood.

Diet and environment can also impact the vibrancy of your goldfish. You can even buy special colour enhancing diets if you really want to get the brightest fish possible.

Do I need a light for my goldfish tank?

A light in your aquarium will make for a more visually stunning effect and will also enhance the colour of your goldfish. Bear in mind though that a light can actually heat up the water temperature, so make sure it isn't having an adverse affect by checking the temperature regularly, and switching it off after a few hours.

Can I handle my goldfish?

It's best that you don't handle your goldfish, although you may see pictures of breeders doing so. These delicate creatures aren't designed for human handling, and can lose the important slime covering on their scales as a result. This leaves them vulnerable to infection. When you need to transfer your goldfish to another tank, use a net instead.

I heard that I can leave my fish without food while I go on holiday. Is this true?

Goldfish can survive for long periods without food, but obviously only if absolutely necessary. If you can't find someone to drop in and feed your fish while you're away, they should be fine without food for a week or so, but no longer than that.

How long will my goldfish live for, realistically?

That depends on how well you look after your goldfish, and whether they came from a good quality breeder or pet shop. If all goes well they could live for anything between ten to fifteen years, though there are some records of fish living for 40 years. Amazing!

Can I introduce a new goldfish to my existing aquarium?

Yes, you can add a new fish provided it is a variety that is compatible with the fish already there. Experts recommend that you quarantine the new fish for at least two weeks before adding it to your aquarium. This will make sure that the new fish isn't bringing in any diseases with it from the fishery where it was raised.

Can I breed my goldfish?

If you're a beginner goldfish keeper, you should wait a while until you know enough to start breeding. It is a delicate, complex business and not one you can just leave up to mother nature. Breeding goldfish need excellent standards of care, and they also need specific temperature changes in the tank to induce breeding. At the very least, you will need an extra, slightly smaller tank for the "fry" (the baby fish), a water filter and a heater so that you can easily change the water temperature. You'll need to induce mating by raising the temperature of the tank and when you see white spots appearing on the gills of the males, you'll know that they are ready to mate.

The males will then chase the females around the tank and nudge their bellies. When the females are ready they will lay eggs, and the male will then fertilise them. Once this has happened you need to move the eggs to your second tank, because goldfish in captivity will actually eat their own eggs otherwise. You can do this by gently removing the entire plant or object that the eggs have been laid on.

Then you need to wait for them to hatch into fry. They will stay at the bottom of the tank for the first few days but when they start swimming around the tank, you'll know it's time to feed them. This is a very brief description of what happens when breeding goldfish. If you decide to do it, you should ask your local aquatic specialist for advice.

What should I feed baby fish?

Newly hatched fry will be too small to eat regular fish food. Instead, you can feed them tiny bits of the yolk from a hard boiled egg. You can dissolve some small bits in a small jar of tank water first, by adding small crumbs and shaking the jar of water and then slowly adding it to the tank for them to feed on the small particles.

What is the ideal temperature for my goldfish tank?

Your goldfish need a water temperature of between 64 and 74 degrees Fahrenheit.

What is the ideal pH for my goldfish tank?

Your goldfish need water with a pH level of 7.2 to 7.6. To get this right, you can buy a testing kit from most aquarium shops.

What is water cycling and do I need to do it?

Water cycling refers to the process of getting the water conditions exactly right, in terms of having enough friendly bacteria to adequately deal with your fish's ammonia production. Serious goldfish keepers swear by it, and it is one way to ensure that your new goldfish get off to the best possible start.

During water cycling, you need to add various amounts of ammonia to the water and then test it to see if any nitrites are being produced. If they are, it is a sign that you are starting to cultivate some friendly bacteria.

You need to keep adding ammonia and testing the water until you see zero ammonia levels, zero nitrite levels and some nitrate levels. This will signify that your tank has enough friendly bacteria in it to successfully convert the ammonia (which can be toxic to your fish if it builds up) into the much safer substance known as nitrate.

If this sounds a little bit too scientific for you, don't worry – go and have a chat with your local aquatic specialist and they will provide you with a testing kit, and a guide as to how to proceed.

Whether or not you "need" to do it is debatable, but it is definitely going to be hugely beneficial to your new goldfish.

What are some of the biggest mistakes made by goldfish owners?

There are lots of mistakes you can make as goldfish are such delicate creatures. However, some of the biggest and most serious mistakes include:

- Not preparing the water in the aquarium before the arrival of your fish
- Buying a tank that is too small for the number of fish you have bought
- Putting your goldfish in a state of shock, by changing the temperature of their water suddenly
- Cleaning the tank too much, and removing the vital friendly bacteria
- Handling your goldfish, thereby removing the slimy protective layer on the scales
- Overfeeding your fish and making them ill as a result
- Forgetting to treat tap water to remove the chlorine before you add it to your aquarium
- Buying fish from a pet shop that keeps their fish in poor conditions or has diseases in their aquariums
- Putting the wrong kinds of goldfish together in an aquarium, resulting in some fish not getting enough food or being bullied by other fish
- Putting your goldfish in an bowl, which will not give them enough oxygen and will be very confined for them
- Failing to take action at the first sign of illness, leading to infections spreading to all fish in the aquarium, or even the death of your fish

Conclusion

That brings us to the end of the book – hopefully you've enjoyed reading about these wonderful pets. Basic goldfish care is not complicated, as long as you are consistent with feeding and cleaning, and you remain vigilant for any signs of illness. Vet's fees for goldfish are relatively inexpensive, so don't be afraid to report anything unusual to your vet. He or she will be only too happy to help you get your fish back to health.

You should now be feeling a lot more confident, and even more excited about becoming a goldfish enthusiast. One thing is for sure, it is going to be a very rewarding and fascinating journey for you and your family. Whether you're going to be keeping just a few fish or a large aquarium, your goldfish will certainly be a talking point for visitors to your home and will provide many happy hours of entertainment as you watch them grow.

Over time you will become a more experienced goldfish keeper and you might decide to keep lots of different varieties of fish. You might even get a second aquarium, or choose to keep some goldfish in your garden pond. Many goldfish enthusiasts started out like you, unsure but willing to learn. Eventually they became passionate about these stunning creatures and some even became breeders.

The sheer popularity of the goldfish and the number of goldfish enthusiasts around the world is one of the reasons why we have so many wonderful varieties today. It is fascinating to think that all of these vastly different goldfish descended from the same wild carp once upon a time.

Lastly, don't forget that goldfish are said to be therapeutic and can add a calming element to any environment, which is just one of the many ways your little fish will reward you. They are also a fantastic way to teach young children about the complexities of looking after another living thing, and can teach them a great deal about responsibility, biology and animal welfare.

In fact, goldfish these days can be a great addition to classrooms, not to mention restaurants, work places, and waiting rooms – anywhere their beauty and exuberance can be appreciated.

That is not to say that they should be purely decorative features – on the contrary, you should always remember that your goldfish are real, complex creatures that, as we have discussed here, need a delicate balance of care to stay healthy. Please remember to feed your goldfish an interesting, varied diet that includes some treats now and then they will thank you for it by becoming brighter and healthier than ever.

Don't forget to pay close attention to their living conditions by testing their water to make sure it's the right temperature and pH. Doing this Is the key to happy, healthy goldfish and a thriving aquarium. It will also set you apart from the many goldfish owners out there who forget to put the welfare of their fish first. Let's not forget that myth that we talked about in Chapter 1 – the myth of the three second goldfish memory.

Goldfish live for longer than most other small pets you can buy in a pet shop, and we know that they can remember things for at least three months, as well as recognise people's faces. This makes them pretty fascinating pets!

With that said, however many goldfish you choose to keep, may you have many happy years together.

Want to know more about looking after your pet?

The writer of this book, Dr. Gordon Roberts, is a veterinarian and owns a total of eight animal hospitals around the UK. He believes that the key to a healthy, happy pet is preventative care, which is only possible when pet owners take the initiative to educate themselves about their animals. As a result, Gordon has written dozens of useful reports on pet care in order to share his years of experience with discerning pet owners. As a thank you for purchasing this book, you can browse and download his specialist reports completely free of charge! You'll learn all sorts of useful information about how to spot possible health conditions early on, and how to make preventative care for your pet a priority, helping you save time and money on visits to the vet later on. To view and download these bonus reports, simply visit Gordon's website at: http://drgordonroberts.com/freereportsdownload/.

Best wishes,
Gordon

Printed in Great Britain
by Amazon

12180869R00029